Show Me a Story

Visual Aids for Telling Bible Stories

Anita Reith Stohs
Illustrated by Michelle Dorenkamp

CONCORDIA PUBLISHING HOUSE • SAINT LOUIS

Contents

Introduction
4

Storytelling Techniques...
Book, Diorama, Flannelgraph, Large Storytelling Tube, Magnet Board, Magnetic Puzzle, Overhead Projector
5

PowerPoint, Puppets
6

Scroll, Storytelling Glove, Tube Puppet Stage, TV Screen, Velcro Apron, Velcro Storyboard
7

Bible Story Index
64

Published by Concordia Publishing House
3558 S. Jefferson Avenue, St. Louis, MO 63118-3968
1-800-325-3040 • www.cph.org

All rights reserved. Unless specifically noted, no part of this publication may be reproduced, stored in a retrieval system, or transmitted, in any form or by any means, electronic, mechanical, photocopying, recording, or otherwise, without the prior written permission of Concordia Publishing House.

The purchaser of this publication is allowed to reproduce the marked portions contained herein for use in the classroom and to send home for parents to use with children. These resources may not be transferred or copied to another user.

Text copyright © 2004 Anita Reith Stohs
Illustrations copyright © 2004 Concordia Publishing House

Scripture quotations are taken from the HOLY BIBLE, NEW INTERNATIONAL VERSION®. NIV®. Copyright © 1973, 1978, 1984 by International Bible Society. Used by permission of Zondervan Publishing House. All rights reserved.

Songs as noted are taken from *Sing-Along Praise*, Anita Reith Stohs. Copyright © 1999 by Concordia Publishing House. All rights reserved.

This publication may be available in braille, in large print, or on cassette tape for the visually impaired. Please allow 8 to 12 weeks for delivery. Write to the Library for the Blind, 7550 Watson Rd., St. Louis, MO 63119-4409; call toll-free 1-888-215-2455; or visit the Web site: www.blindmission.org.

Manufactured in the United States of America

1 2 3 4 5 6 7 8 9 10   13 12 11 10 09 08 07 06 05 04

Old Testament

God Made Our Wonderful World (Book)	8
Adam and Eve (Storytelling glove)	10
God Saves Noah (Stand-up figures)	12
Abraham and Sarah (Magnet board)	14
Joseph and His Brothers (Stick puppets)	16
Baby Moses (Velcro apron)	18
The First Passover (Finger puppets)	20
Miriam's Song of Praise (Round container puppet)	22
Ten Commandments (Storytelling tube)	24
Naaman and the Servant Girl (Velcro board)	26
Daniel in the Lions' Den (Stuffed Velcro figures)	28

New Testament

The Birth of John the Baptist (Scroll)	30
Jesus Is Born (Tube puppets)	32
Angels and Shepherds (Flannelgraph)	34
The Coming of the Wise Men (TV screen)	36
Jesus' Baptism (Cup puppets)	38
Jesus Blesses the Children (Velcro apron)	40
Feeding the Five Thousand (Stick puppets)	42
Jesus and Zacchaeus (Stand-up puppets)	44
The Ten Lepers (Storytelling tube)	46
The Good Neighbor (Cup puppets)	48
Palm Sunday (Book)	50
The Last Supper (Scroll)	52
Garden of Gethsemane (Movable strip diorama)	54
Good Friday (Overhead projector)	56
Easter Morning (Magnet board)	58
Ascension (Hanging puppets)	60
Pentecost (Magnetic puzzle)	62

To Laura Podrebarac, Denise Vertz, Marilyn Peter, Ruth Taylor, and Edna Blanz, in recognition for the years in which they have taught the Good News of Jesus' saving love to the little children in their classes, showing them "the praiseworthy deeds of the LORD, His power, and the wonders He has done."
Psalm 78:4–7

Introduction

One of my earliest memories of Sunday school is of one I visited in the small Iowa town in which my family had once lived. My one vivid memory of that visit is seeing a flannelgraph for the first (and only) time in my Sunday school experience and getting to help put on the pieces that illustrated the day's Bible story.

For me, this experience has always been an example of how much we remember what we see and do. When children combine visual and auditory experiences, they remember more and for a longer period of time. This book was written to provide religious education teachers with storytelling techniques that will involve their students in lifelong Bible learning such as this.

Using This Book

★ With the help of readily available materials, such as flannel, felt, magnets, Velcro, paper, markers, crayons, and glue, storytelling pictures can be adapted to a wide variety of storytelling techniques.

★ A specific technique is suggested for each Bible story included in this book, but options for other ways to use the teaching pictures are included.

★ Story scripts can be read by the teacher or students and are written to be adapted as needed to your classroom size and student reading level. For example, if the interactive responses in a script are not appropriate for your students' age and reading level, use straight narration.

★ Optional prayers or songs are also included at the end of each script to provide students with a way to respond to the story they have heard.

Storytelling Tips and Pointers

★ Use a photocopier to enlarge or reduce shapes to meet your storytelling needs.

★ Use markers or crayons to color larger shapes and fine-tipped markers or colored pencils for small shapes and figures.

★ Consider enlisting students to help you make storytelling shapes.

★ Have a set of visual aids in an accessible area in your classroom for pre-session activities.

★ Keep a set of teaching shapes for key Bible stories to use with visiting children who have not yet heard of Jesus' love and forgiveness for them.

★ Have students make their own storytelling aids as a way to both reinforce the lesson and to share Bible stories with others outside the classroom.

★ Storytelling techniques found in this book can also be adapted to teach hymns, Bible verses, books of the Bible, key points in a lesson, and a wide variety of other lesson-related uses.

★ Although figures are provided for quick and easy Bible story visual aids, be creative in obtaining figures from other sources such as Bible story leaflets, the Internet, stickers, and coloring books. Or, encourage the children in your class to draw the storytelling figures you will use.

Use the shapes and techniques in this book with other Bible stories you teach as you reach out more effectively with the Good News of Jesus, our Savior, to the students in your class. May God bless your service in Jesus' name!

The Author

Storytelling Techniques

Book

For small to medium-sized groups, depending upon book size.

1. Stack several flannel or felt rectangles in a pile. Sew them along the middle and fold to make a book.
2. For each page, glue on paper pictures or other pieces of fabric for background details. Draw pictures with markers or fabric paint.
3. As an option, store storytelling shapes to be attached with Velcro or flannel in an envelope at the back of the book. Add the shapes as you turn the pages.

Diorama

Use the diorama as a visual aid when teaching stories with little action to small groups.

1. Cut out the side of a box and decorate the inside with construction paper.
2. Cut out storytelling figures, leaving an extra tab at the bottom.
3. Fold back the tab at the bottom of the figure and glue it in place.
4. Point to the figures as you tell the story.
5. As an option, stand up figures with a ring of paper glued to the back of the figures.

Flannelgraph

For small to medium-sized groups, depending upon the size of the figures.

1. Make a storyboard by gluing a piece of flannel or felt to a piece of foam core or corrugated cardboard. Color in background detail.
2. Cut felt into shapes that illustrate the story. If desired, use markers to add details. Or glue flannel, felt, or sandpaper to the back of the teaching shapes.
3. Position the storytelling shapes or pictures on the flannel board as you tell the story.

Large Storytelling Tube

For small to medium-sized groups.

1. Cover the outside of a large, round container, such as an oatmeal box.
2. Glue sets of pictures around the tube.
3. Turn the tube as you tell the part of the story that the figures on the tube represent.

Magnet Board

For small to medium-sized groups, depending upon the size of the figures.

1. Glue lightweight cardboard or poster board behind each storytelling shape for stability.
2. Glue a magnet square to the back of the shape.
3. Position the shape on a magnet board or cookie sheet as you tell the story, Bible passage, or hymn verse.

Magnetic Puzzle

For small to medium-sized groups, depending upon the size of the pieces.

1. Cut a Bible story picture into puzzle pieces. Option: use a commercial Bible story puzzle.
2. Glue a magnet square to the back of each puzzle piece.
3. Place the pieces on a magnetic board as you tell the story.

Overhead Projector

For any size group.

1. Cut shapes from dark paper.
2. Place shapes on the overhead projector to tell the story.

PowerPoint

For any size group.
1. Draw pictures or glue down figures to illustrate a story. Option: print and paste in pictures from the Internet.
2. Scan the pictures to be used for a PowerPoint presentation.
3. Add narration, Bible passages, prayers, and songs.

Puppets

For small to large groups, depending upon the size of the puppets.
1. Copy, color, and cut out the puppet figures you need to tell your Bible story.
2. Laminate the figures or glue them to poster board.

Container Puppets

For small groups.
1. Draw a scene on a strip of paper and glue it around a round container.
2. Option: fill container with beans and glue on lid.
3. Move the container around as you tell the story.

Cup Puppets

For small groups.
1. Turn a paper or foam cup upside down and glue a figure to its side.
2. Move the cup around a table as you tell the story.
3. Option: glue a craft stick inside the cup to turn it into a stick puppet
4. Option: glue a shape to the end of a stick and pop it up from the inside of the cup.

Stick Puppets

For small to medium-sized groups, depending upon the size of the puppets.
1. Glue a stick behind each paper figure.
2. Hold the puppet by the stick to tell the story.

Stand-up Puppets

For small to medium-sized groups, depending upon the size of the puppets.
1. Cut a paper strip and glue the ends to make a ring.
2. Glue paper ring to the base of the puppet to stand it up.
3. Use a box or a table top for a stage.

Finger Puppets

For small groups.
1. Cut a paper strip to fit your finger.
2. Glue a shape onto the strip or draw a figure directly onto the paper strip.

Movable Puppet Strips

For small groups.
1. Decorate the inside of a box.
2. Glue puppets to one end of a strip of cardboard and move the puppets around as you tell the story.

Tube Puppets

For small groups.
1. Cut a paper rectangle.
2. Glue a figure to the center of the rectangle.
3. Glue the sides of the rectangle to make a tube and stand it up.

Hanging Puppets

For small to medium-sized groups, depending upon the size of the puppets.
1. Glue a piece of yarn to each puppet.
2. Move the figures from the top of the box as you tell a story, or tie the yarn to a dowel to move the figures.

Scroll

For small to medium-size groups, depending upon the size of the scroll.
1. Glue storytelling shapes to a long sheet of paper.
2. Glue each end of the paper to a dowel.
3. Roll the sides of the scroll inward.
4. Unroll the scroll as you tell the story.

Storytelling Glove

For small groups.
1. Cut storytelling shapes from felt or glue a commercial Bible story sticker or paper picture to a piece of felt.
2. Option: make faces from pom-pom balls, felt, and yarn.
3. Attach one side of Velcro to the fingertips of a garden glove and the other side to the backs of storytelling shapes.
4. After you have used your glove to tell a Bible story, give it to the students to use in telling the story to someone else.

Tube Puppet Stage

For small groups.
1. Glue figures to strips of paper.
2. Glue the strips around a narrow tube and turn the figures around as you tell the story.

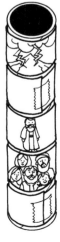

TV Screen

For small groups.
1. Glue storytelling shapes to a roll of paper to make a scroll.
2. Cut out one side of a cardboard box.
3. Poke dowels through the box sides at each side of the hole.
4. Glue the ends of the storytelling scroll to the dowels and wind the pictures past the "TV screen."

Velcro Apron

For small groups.
1. Make an apron from felt or a type of fabric to which "hooked" Velcro adheres. Add a large pocket at the bottom of the apron for holding storytelling pieces.
2. Option: use fabric glue to attach a piece of fabric or felt to the front of a commercially made apron. Or cut a hole for your head in the center of a length of felt and fit it over your head for a poncho apron.
3. Cut storytelling pieces from felt or paper. (Laminate or back with lightweight cardboard or felt for more stability.)
4. Option: make stuffed fabric figures.
5. Attach pieces of Velcro to the back of fabric shapes.
6. Store the shapes in the apron pocket until you use them, then attach them to the apron front as you tell the story.

Velcro Storyboard

For small to medium-sized groups.
1. Glue a piece of felt, or any fabric to which Velcro will attach, onto a piece of corrugated or foam core.
2. Option: make small, stuffed figures of Bible story characters.
3. Glue Velcro to the back of each storytelling shape or picture.
4. Attach the Velcro-backed shapes to the board as you tell the story.

Book

God Made Our Wonderful World
Genesis 1:1–2:25

Pattern
Fold two felt rectangles together. Glue along the center to make a spine. Use fabric paint to write the words "It Was Very Good" on the cover. Copy, color, and glue each picture to a page.

Storytelling Options
Glue circles to craft sticks for stick puppets or to Velcro to go on a storytelling glove. Or use Internet pictures to make a PowerPoint presentation.

Tell the Story

Have the children respond with the words, "It was very good," as you turn the pages of the book.

Reader: In the beginning, God created the heavens and the earth. On the first day, God said, "Let there be light." And there was light. God made day and night.

All: It was very good.

Reader: On the second day, God made sky and water.

All: It was very good.

Reader: On the third day, God made dry land and separated it from the water. God made plants and trees.

All: It was very good.

Reader: On the fourth day, God made the sun, moon, and stars.

All: It was very good.

Reader: On the fifth day, God made fish and birds.

All: It was very good.

Reader: On the sixth day, God made animals and God made Adam in His image.

All: It was very good.

Reader: God made Eve to live with Adam.

All: It was very good.

Song: "God Made All Things"

Tune: "Are You Sleeping?"

God made all things,
God made all things,
Earth and sky, earth and sky.
_____ and _____ and _____.
_____ and _____ and _____.
It was good; it was good.

Prayer

Dear Father in heaven, with Your Son Jesus You created everything in this world—including me. Thank You for creating all the good things in this world. I especially want to thank You for making me Your child in Baptism. Forgive me when I fail to thank You for giving me everything I have.
I pray this in Jesus' name. Amen.

Storytelling Glove

Adam and Eve
Genesis 3:1-20

Storytelling Glove Set

Copy and cut out these circles and glue each to poster board or felt. Glue a piece of hooked Velcro to the back of each circle. Glue a piece of smooth Velcro to the fingertip of each glove. As the story is told, place the appropriate circles on the glove fingertips.

Storytelling Option

Glue circles to plastic cups to make tabletop puppets.

Tell the Story

Add circles to fingertips as the story is read. Wiggle fingers a bit as the circle picture is mentioned in the story. Let children read different parts for a story review.

(Start with God circle on thumb.)
(Add Adam and Eve circles to next two fingers.) God made a beautiful garden for Adam and Eve.
(Add tree circle to ring finger.) God put many trees in His garden. "Eat from any tree in the garden," God said, "except from the tree of the knowledge of good and evil. If you do so, you will die."
(Add snake circle to little finger and bend down thumb with God circle.) One day the devil took the shape of a snake and came to Eve. "Did God really say not to eat from any tree in the garden?" asked the snake.
(Move Eve circle.) "God said we could eat fruit from any tree in the garden," Eve said, "except from the tree of the knowledge of good and evil. If we do, we'll die."
(Move snake circle.) "You won't die!" the snake lied. "You will know good from evil. You will be like God!"
(Bend down snake circle. Move Eve circle.) Eve looked at the fruit and saw that it looked good. She ate it. "Here, eat some too," she said to Adam. And he did.
(Move then bend down the fingers with Adam and Eve circles.) Adam and Eve saw that they had no clothes. They sewed some clothes from fig leaves and put them on. Then they heard God coming. They hid.
(Bring up God circle.) "Where are you?" asked God.
(Bring up Adam and Eve circles.) "I heard you and was afraid," Adam said. "I had no clothes so I hid."
(Move God circle.) "Who told you that you had no clothes?" asked God. "Did you eat from the tree I said not to eat from?"
(Move Adam circle.) "Eve gave me the fruit and I ate it," Adam said.
(Move Eve circle.) "The snake tricked me," said Eve.
Because they disobeyed God, Adam and Eve had to leave the beautiful garden God had made for them. But God still loved them and promised that a Savior would come—Jesus, the seed of the woman, who died to forgive the sins of Adam, Eve, and all people.

Song: "Forgiveness Is a Gift"

Tune: "The Old Gray Mare"
Forgiveness is a gift of the Lord to me,
Gift of the Lord to me,
Gift of the Lord to me.
Forgiveness is a gift of the Lord to me,
A gift of grace so free.

(from *Sing-Along Praise*)

Prayer

Thank You, God, for forgiving our sins for Jesus' sake. Amen.

Stand-Up Figures

God Saves Noah
Genesis 6:1—8:22

Storytelling Set

Copy, color, and cut out the figures shown here. Cut the end from each side of a small cereal box. Cover the back of the box with blue paper and the other side with gray. Glue an ark to each side. On the blue side of the box, glue a strip of green paper below the ark. On the gray side, glue a strip of waves below the ark. Cut two slits into the side of the box for the rainbow to fit in. Glue a paper ring to the back of each figure to stand it up.

Storytelling Options

Use figures for a flannel, magnet, or Velcro board.

Tell the Story

First tell the story without the response as you place the figures on the table in front of you. For a story review, tell the story again, having the children respond with the appropriate words.

(Put out Noah shape.)
Reader: God said to Noah, "Build a big, big boat."
All: And Noah did.
(Put out ark shape, with the grass facing the children.)
Reader: God said to Noah, "Take two of every kind of animal into the boat."
All: And Noah did.
(Move animal strip inside box.)
Reader: God said to Noah, "Take your family inside the boat."
All: And Noah did.
(Move strip with Noah's family inside the box.)
Reader: It rained and rained for forty days and nights.
(Turn box around to show side with rain.)
Reader: Noah trusted in God to keep him and his family safe.
All: And God did.

Reader: The rain stopped. God said to Noah, "Come out of the boat."
All: And Noah did.
(Remove all figures from inside the box.)
Reader: Noah built an altar and thanked God for keeping him safe. God said He would put a rainbow in the sky as a sign that there would never again destroy the earth with a flood.
(Add rainbow.)
All: And God did.

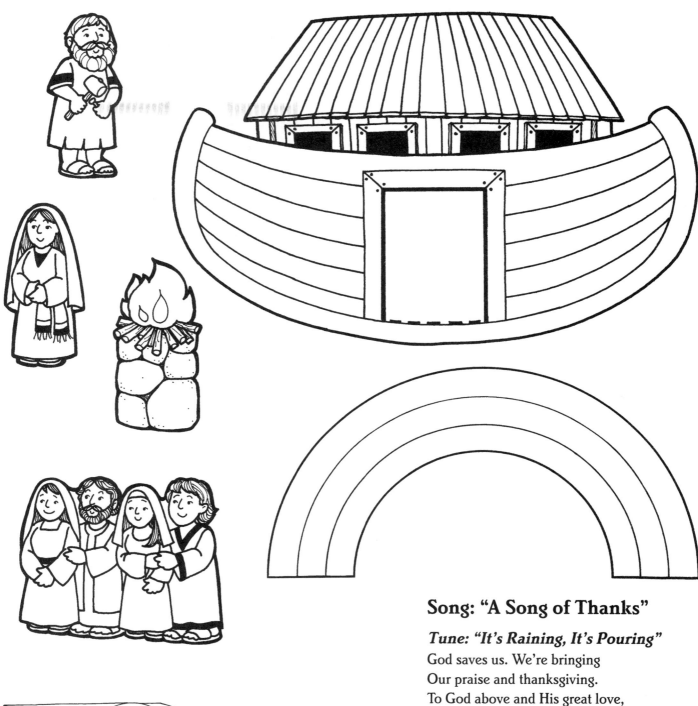

Song: "A Song of Thanks"

Tune: "It's Raining, It's Pouring"
God saves us. We're bringing
Our praise and thanksgiving.
To God above and His great love,
A song of thanks we're singing.
(from *Sing-Along Praise*)

Prayer
Lord, You keep Your promises, especially Your promise to send us a Savior from our sin. We believe that You love us and for Jesus' sake will forgive us for the times we don't trust You to keep us safe. Amen.

Old Testament Story

Magnet Board

Abraham and Sarah
Genesis 17:1-9, 15-19; 18:1-15; 21:1-7

Storytelling Set
Copy, color, and cut out the figures, then glue them to poster board. Glue a magnet behind each figure. Position them on a cookie sheet.

Storytelling Option
Glue figures to paper cups to make stand-up puppets to move across a table.

Tell the Story

Add the figures to a cookie sheet while you tell the story without responses. Have children take turns reading parts and repeating the phrase "God keeps His promises" for a story review.

(Add figure for Abraham and tell the story from his perspective.)
Abraham: "Leave your country," God told me, "and go to the land I will show you. Your name will be great and you will be a blessing."
All: God keeps His promises.
(Add Sarah figure and move the two figures across the background.)
Abraham: "My wife Sarah and I went to faraway Canaan. Many years passed and Sarah and I still had no children."
All: God keeps His promises.
(Add several stars.)
Abraham: One night God spoke to me again. "Look at the sky and count the stars. You will have as many children as the stars."
All: God keeps His promises.
(Remove the stars.)
Abraham: Many years passed and still Sarah and I had no children. God spoke to me again, "Sarah will have a son. She will be the mother of many nations."
All: God keeps His promises.
(Add three men.)
Abraham: One day at noon, three men came near my tent. "Stop and eat," I told them. One was the Lord, and the other two were angels. "You will have a son," the Lord told me.
All: God keeps His promises.
Abraham: Sarah heard and laughed. "How can this be," she thought. "I'm too old to have a baby!"
But the Lord knew what she was thinking and said, "Why did Sarah laugh? Is anything too hard for the Lord?"
All: God keeps His promises.
(Put up figure of Sarah holding a baby.)
Abraham: God kept His promise. Sarah and I had a baby boy, and we called him "Isaac," which means "laughter."
All: God keeps His promises.

Song: "Father Abraham"

Prayer

Dear Father, forgive me for the times I broke my promises. Thank You for being my faithful God who kept His promise to give Abraham a son and through his family gave me a Savior so I would be able to laugh in heaven. Amen.

Stick Puppets

Joseph and His Brothers
Genesis 37:1-36

Storytelling Set
Color and cut out the puppets, then glue them to craft sticks.

Storytelling Option
Glue paper rings to each figure to turn them into movable, stand-up figures.

Song: "Show God's Love"

Tune: "Skip to My Lou"

Show God's love in all you do.
Show God's love in all you do.
Show God's love in all you do,
In what you say and what you do.

Show God's love in all you say.
Show God's love in all you say.
Show God's love in all you say,
In what you do and what you say.

(from *Sing-Along Praise*)

Tell the Story

Have children hold the puppets as you read the story. Divide the reading parts among students for a story review. Use a paper cup for the well.

Parts: Reader, Joseph, Reuben, Judah, brothers, and Jacob. Nonreading parts are other brothers and traders.

(The Joseph puppet with a coat is held up first; the Joseph puppet without the coat is held up after he is thrown into the well.)

Reader: Jacob had twelve sons, but he loved Joseph best of all. One day he gave Joseph a robe with many colors. Did the brothers like that?

Brothers: No!

Reader: Joseph told his brothers a dream.

Joseph: Your bundles of grain bowed down to mine.

Reader: Joseph had another dream.

Joseph: The sun, the moon, and eleven stars bowed down to me.

Reader: Did his brothers like these dreams?

Brothers: No!

Reader: One day, Jacob's sons were in the field watching their sheep. Jacob sent Joseph to see how they were doing.

Brothers: Look, Joseph is coming. Let's kill him. That will take care of his dreams.

Reader: But Reuben wanted to save his brother.

Reuben: Do not kill Joseph. Just put him into a well.

Reader: Reuben left. He planned to come back later to save Joseph. The other brothers took off Joseph's beautiful robe and threw him into the well.

Then some traders came by. Joseph's brother Judah said:

Judah: Let us not kill Joseph. Sell him to the traders instead.

Reader: The traders bought Joseph and took him to Egypt. The brothers tore Joseph's robe and dipped it into goat blood. Then they took it to their father.

Brothers: We found this. Is it your son's robe?

Reader: Jacob thought wild animals had killed his son and he was sad for many days. But God turned the evil the brothers had done to good. Joseph grew up and became an important leader. Many years later, with God's help, Joseph forgave his brothers and gave them food when they had none.

Prayer

Lord God, Joseph forgave his brothers for hating him and trying to kill him. When we sin by being angry or disliking someone like Joseph's brothers did, Jesus forgives us. Turn our hearts to godly penitence, and forgive us for Jesus' sake. Teach us to love others as You have loved us. In Jesus' name. Amen.

Velcro Apron

Baby Moses
Exodus 2:1-10

Storytelling Set
Color and cut out the pieces shown here. Glue them to a piece of poster board or felt and cut out. Glue a piece of hooked Velcro to the back of each figure. Use a commercial Velcro apron or make one from polyester fabric.

Storytelling Option
Use a shoebox to make a diorama.

Tell the Story

Add storytelling pieces to the apron as you tell the story. Divide the story into parts for a review.

After Joseph died, God's people lived in Egypt for many years. Then a man who did not like God's people became king. This bad king made the people his slaves and wanted to kill their baby boys.

(Add Moses' mother holding baby.) One day a little boy named Moses was born.

"I love the baby God has given me," said Moses' mother. "I will hide him and keep him safe." But Moses grew bigger and bigger, and his mother could no longer hide him.

(Add basket below Baby Moses.) "I know what I will do," Moses' mother said. "I'll make a basket and cover it with tar so it will float." And she did.

(Add Miriam.) Moses' mother called her daughter, Miriam, and said, "I will put Moses in this basket boat and hide it in the river grasses. I want you to hide there too and watch to see that he is safe."

(Remove Moses' mother. Add grasses and Moses in basket.) Miriam carefully watched her brother as he floated in the basket.

(Add princess and servants.) Soon the Egyptian princess and her servants came to the river.

Moses began to cry.

"What is that sound? Go and see what it is," the princess told her servants. They went to see.

"It's a baby!" the servants said.

"Bring it to me," said the princess, and they did.

(Place Moses in basket next to princess.) "What a beautiful baby," said the princes. "I want to keep him. But how will I take care of a baby?"

"I know a woman who can take care of him," said Miriam. "Let me get her."

(Remove basket with Moses. Add Moses' mother holding baby.) Miriam ran and brought her mother to the princess.

"I will pay you to take this baby home and care for him until he is big enough to live with me in the palace," said the princess.

So Moses' mother took Moses back home and took care of him when he was little. When Moses grew up, God used him to lead His people out of Egypt and to give them His Ten Commandments.

Song: "Sleep, Little Moses"

Tune: "Hush, Little Baby"
Sleep, little Moses, don't say a word.
God, your mother's prayer has heard.
He will guard you as you float
In your little basket boat.

Prayer

Lord Jesus Christ, as You delivered the children of Israel out of slavery in Egypt, You also delivered us from slavery to sin. Thank You for being our Savior. Help us, Your penitent and forgiven people, to serve You with joy as did Moses and his family. In Your name we pray. Amen.

Finger Puppets

The First Passover
Exodus 11:1-16

Storytelling Set
Copy, color, and cut out the puppets. Glue them to fit around your fingertips. Put the puppets on your fingers and move them as you tell the story.

Storytelling Option
Use puppet faces on a storytelling glove.

Tell the Story
Place the father finger puppet on your thumb and children finger puppets on the other fingers. Move fingers as different puppets speak.

Father: Tonight will be a special night. God is going to set us free from being slaves in Egypt. Remember the things God did to make Pharaoh let us go?

The waters became blood, frogs hopped about, dust turned to gnats, flies buzzed and bit, and animals died. And still Pharaoh said:

All: No!

Father: What other things did God do?

Children: Boils hurt, hail fell, locusts swarmed, and darkness fell.

Father: And still Pharaoh said:

Children: No!

Father: Tonight will be a special night. Moses told us to kill a lamb and to paint the outside of our door with the blood of the lamb. We are to bake bread quickly and eat a special meal. We must be ready to leave Egypt this very night.

Child: The angel of death moves through the town.

Mother: But the blood of the lamb saves us. And Pharaoh finally says:

All: Go!

Father: The angel of death has passed over us. We are free.

All: God set us free!

Mother: The Lord wants us to remember this night because He protected us. We will call this night "Passover."

All: Praise God!

Reader: Jesus is our Passover Lamb, whose blood set us free.

All: Amen!

Song: "God Loves Us"

Tune: "Three Blind Mice"
God is love. God is love.
   (Point up.)
God loves you. God loves me.
   (Point to others, then to self.)
God loved us so much
That He sent His own Son,
   (Pretend to rock baby.)
Who died on the cross
To forgive everyone.
   (Make cross with fingers.)
God is love. God is love.
   (Point up.)

(from *Sing-Along Praise*)

Prayer

God in heaven, You set the children of Israel free from Pharaoh and You set us free from sin by sending Jesus to earn our forgiveness. Jesus is the Passover Lamb who is the sacrifice for our sin. Thank You, God. Amen.

Round Container Puppet

Miriam's Song of Praise
Exodus 15:1-21

Storytelling Set
Copy, color, and cut out the figure of Miriam. Glue it around a small can with a plastic lid. Add several beans or jingle bells before gluing on the lid.

Storytelling Options
Glue the shape to a cup or craft stick.

Prayer

Dear Lord Jesus, Moses led God's people out of slavery and into the Promised Land. You freed us from our slavery to sin by Your sacrificial death. Thank You, Jesus, for making us free to live as children of God. Amen.

Tell the Story

Move the puppet as you tell the story without responses. Shake it as you sing Miriam's song of praise. Have the students help read it for a storytelling review, adding movements to fit the responses.

Miriam: Hurrah! God has brought us out of Egypt. We are on our way to the Promised Land. Oh no! Look at all the water. We have come to the Red Sea. What will we do?

All: What will we do?

Miriam: What is brother Moses doing? He's holding out his hands.

All: He's holding out his hands.

Miriam: Listen, I hear a loud wind!

All: I hear a loud wind!

Miriam: God sent a big wind to pull apart the Red Sea's waters. Listen, I hear footsteps!

All: I hear footsteps!

Miriam: The children of Israel are walking on the dry path through the middle of the sea. Let's go too.

All: Let's go too.

Miriam: On no! I hear horses.

All: I hear horses.

Miriam: Pharaoh is sending soldiers to take us back to Egypt. Who will help? God will help!

All: God will help!

Miriam: We made it to the other side. But wait. I hear the water roar!

All: I hear the water roar!

Miriam: The waters are falling back. We are safe! Praise God!

All: Praise God!

Song: "Sing unto the Lord"

Tune: "Row, Row, Row Your Boat"

> Come sing unto the Lord,
> Join in and sing along!
> Our salvation is the Lord,
> He is our strength and song.

Old Testament Story

Storytelling Tube

Ten Commandments
Deuteronomy 5:1-22

Storytelling Set

Copy and color the strips. Glue the strips around a cardboard tube in the following order, from bottom to top: golden calf, people, Moses without tablets, Moses with tablets, mountain.

Song: "Ten Commandments"

Tune: "Ten Little Indians"

One, and two, and three Commandments,
Four, and five, and six Commandments,
Seven, and eight, and nine Commandments,
God gave Ten Commandments.

Tell the Story

Turn the storytelling strips as directed as you tell the story.

(Turn around people strip.) God's people were on their way to the Promised Land.

(Turn around first Moses strip.) Moses was leading them.

(Turn around mountain strip.) One day they came to a high mountain. On the third day, a cloud covered the mountain.

Lightning flashed. Thunder rumbled. The people heard the sound of a great trumpet and were afraid. Moses told the people to come to the mountain to meet God. Smoke came from the mountain and the earth shook. God spoke to them:

"I am the Lord your God who brought you out of Egypt, out of the land of slavery.

Do not have any other gods before me.
Do not use God's name in a bad way.
Remember the Sabbath day by keeping it holy.
Honor your father and your mother.
Do not murder.
Do not commit adultery.
Do not steal.
Do not give false testimony against your neighbor.
Do not have a sinful desire for your neighbor's house.
Do not have a sinful desire for your neighbor's family or money."

(Turn back first Moses strip.) The Lord told Moses to come up the mountain.

(Turn around Moses and Ten Commandments strip.) God gave Moses the Ten Commandments written on two tablets for Moses to bring back down the mountain. There Moses saw something that made him very angry.

(Turn around golden calf strip.) The people had made a golden calf for a god. They were dancing around it.

(Turn back Moses and Ten Commandments strip; turn back golden calf.) Moses threw down the tablets of stone that God had given him, and God punished the people who had made the golden calf and worshiped it.

(Turn back Moses and Ten Commandments strip.) Moses went back up the mountain and came back down with the Ten Commandments written on new tablets of stone.

Prayer

Dear God, forgive us for the times we have broken Your commandments. Thank You for loving us anyway and for sending Jesus, who kept the commandments perfectly and saved us from our sins. Amen.

Velcro Board

Naaman and the Servant Girl
2 Kings 10:1-15

Storytelling Set

Copy and color figures, then glue them to poster board. Cut out figures. Glue pieces of hooked Velcro to the back of each one. Cover a piece of cardboard with polyester to make a Velcro board.

Song: "All Who Believe and Are Baptized"

Tell the Story

Add figures as you tell the story without the responses. Have students say the responses for a story review.

Reader: *(Add figure of little girl, Naaman, and his wife.)* A little girl was taken from her home in Israel to be a servant for the wife of an enemy soldier named Naaman. One day Naaman got sick.

All: Poor, poor Naaman!

Reader: The little girl knows who could help Naaman. "If only my master would go to the prophet who lives in my land, Israel," she said. "He would help my master."

All: Go, go Naaman!

Reader: "I will go to Israel," said Naaman. "I will go to the king of Israel."
(Move Naaman to another part of the board and add the king.)

All: No, no, Naaman!

Reader: The king did not know how to help Naaman. He sent Naaman to Elisha.
(Move Naaman to another part of the board and add Elisha figure.)
"Go and dip seven times in the Jordan River," Elisha said.

All: Go, go, Naaman!

Reader: Naaman did not like what Elisha said, "Why should I dip in the little Jordan?" said Naaman. "The rivers at home are better."
"Please go," Naaman's servants said.
And he did. Naaman dipped in the river seven times.
(Move Naaman down and up seven times.)

All: 1-2-3-4-5-6-7.

Reader: Naaman was cured! He went back to his wife and the little servant girl.
(Move Naaman back to where he began.) God had cured Naaman's disease.
Naaman was also brought to faith in the one true God and the promised Messiah—Jesus Christ.

All: Happy, happy Naaman!

Prayer

We pray. Lord God, help us to be always ready to tell others about You and Your great love for them. In Jesus' name. Amen.

Old Testament Story

Stuffed Velcro Figures

Daniel in the Lions' Den
Daniel 6:1-23, 26

Storytelling Set

Enlarge the figures on a photocopier, duplicating as many lions as desired. Color and cut out the figures. Cut out two more shapes from a brown paper bag for each figure. Glue the colored figure to the top paper bag shape and glue the second paper bag shape to the first around the edges, leaving a hole for stuffing. Stuff the bag and glue the hole together. Glue "hooked" Velcro squares to each piece and place them onto a Velcro board made from polyester or knit fabric glued to a piece of corrugated cardboard or foam core.

Song:
"I Am Trusting You, Lord Jesus"

Prayer
God, You are the God who forgives and saves us from sin by Your Son, Jesus Christ.
Help us to trust in Him and pray to Him for help at all times. In Jesus' name. Amen.

Tell the Story

Place shapes on a Velcro board as you tell the story. For a story review, divide the script into parts and have children read responses.

Reader: *(Add Daniel shape.)* In far off Babylon lived an Israelite man named Daniel. Daniel loved God. Three times a day, Daniel—

All: Prayed to God.

Reader: *(Add king shape.)* Daniel was a good servant of the king, but some other servants were jealous of Daniel. They thought of a way to get rid of him.

"O king," they said, "make a law that for thirty days all the people will pray to you. Those who won't pray to you will be thrown into a den of lions."

The king made the new law. When Daniel heard this law, he went to his room and—

All: Prayed to God.

Reader: The jealous servants followed Daniel and saw him pray. Then they went to tell the king.

"O king," they said, "did you not make a law that for thirty days, anyone who prays to any god or man but you will be thrown into a den of lions?"

"I did," said the king.

"Daniel still prays to his God three times a day," said the jealous servants.

The king was unhappy when he heard this. Daniel was put into the den of lions. *(Place lions around Daniel.)*

"May your God save you," said the king. And inside the lions' den, Daniel—

All: Prayed to God.

Reader: The king was worried about Daniel. He could not sleep all night. Early the next morning he went to the lions' den.

"Daniel," the king called," has your God, whom you serve continually, saved you?"

"O king," Daniel answered, "my God sent His angel to shut the mouths of the lions. They have not hurt me."

The king was very happy and had Daniel taken out of the lions' den.

The king made a new law that Daniel's God is the true God, the God who saves.

The king and Daniel—

All: Prayed to God.

Scroll

The Birth of John the Baptist
Luke 1:57-80

Storytelling Set
Make two copies of this page for duplicate figures. Color and cut out figures then glue them to a piece of paper in the following order: Zechariah and altar, angel and Zechariah, people, Elizabeth and baby, Zechariah and tablet. Glue the end of each side of the strip of paper to craft sticks and roll it up.

Storytelling Option
Make a flannel book to use in telling the story.

Song:
"Bless the God of Israel"

Tune: "Skip to my Lou"
Bless the God of Israel;
Bless the God of Israel;
Bless the God of Israel;
Come to save His people.

Tell the Story

Tell the story as you open the scroll. Divide the narration into parts and have children join in the responses for a story review.

Reader: *(Show Zechariah and altar.)* It is the time for prayer in the temple. The people wait while Zechariah prays to God before the altar of incense. Suddenly something wonderful happens. *(Show angel.)*

All: Look. Zechariah, look! An angel has come.

Reader: "Don't be afraid, Zechariah," the angel said. "God has heard your prayer. You and your wife, Elizabeth, will have a son. You will call him John."

All: He will get people ready for the Lord.

Reader: "How can I know that this will be?" asked Zechariah. "My wife and I are old."

"I am Gabriel," the angel said. "God sent me to tell you this good news. But because you did not believe me, you will not be able to speak until the baby God promised you is born."

(Show people.) The people outside the temple wondered what was happening.

All: Where is Zechariah?

Reader: *(Show Zechariah alone.)* When Zechariah came out, he could not speak.

(Show Elizabeth holding baby John.) Nine months later, just as God had promised, Zechariah and his wife, Elizabeth, had a baby boy. When the time came to name the baby, their friends came to their house for a party. *(Show people.)* They said:

All: Name him, Zechariah. Name the baby.

Reader: *(Show Zechariah and tablet.)* Zechariah wrote these words on a tablet, "His name is John."

Once again Zechariah could talk. Join him in his song of praise.

Prayer

Dear Father in heaven, You always keep Your promises. You promised to send a son to Zechariah and Elizabeth and You did. You promised to send a Savior—Your Son—to the world and You did. Forgive us for the times our faith is weak. In Jesus' name we pray. Amen.

New Testament Story

Tube Puppets

Jesus Is Born
Luke 2:1-7

Storytelling Set
Glue each figure to a cardboard tube and make a box stable. Place stable and puppets on a desktop or table. Move puppets as you tell the story.

Storytelling Option
Glue figures to the pages of a felt book.

Song: "Away in a Manger"

Prayer
Jesus, Son of God, we are so happy that You came to save us from our sin. Amen.

Tell the Story

Move the figures as the story is read. First tell the story without the response, then have the children join in for a lesson review. As an option, have the children add motions for each response.

Reader: It is night in Bethlehem. The inns are full of people who have come to their hometown to be counted in the census. It is late, but listen—someone is coming.

All: Step, step, step.

Reader: *(Put out Mary on donkey and Joseph.)* It is Joseph and Mary. They come to an inn and knock at the door.

All: Knock, knock, knock.

Reader: *(Put out innkeeper.)* The innkeeper answers the door to say:

All: "No room, no room."

Reader: There is no room in all of Bethlehem. The only place left is a stable. The innkeeper says:

All: "Stay there, stay there."

Reader: *(Remove Mary on donkey and innkeeper. Add the stable and place Joseph and seated Mary inside it.)* Mary and Joseph went to the stable to sleep.

That night the time came for baby Jesus to be born. *(Add baby Jesus.)* Mary wrapped Him in cloths and placed Him in a manger for a bed.

All: Sleep, Jesus, sleep.

Reader: Jesus, the Savior from sin, is born.

All: Jesus, our God, is born.

Reader: God's promise of a Savior from sin, first given to Adam and Eve, was fulfilled when Jesus was born.

All: Jesus, our Savior, is born.

Flannelgraph

Angels and Shepherds
Luke 2:8-20

Storytelling Set
Copy, color, and cut out the figures. Cut pieces of felt or flannel and glue them to the back of the figures. Glue dark blue felt to a piece of cardboard to make a flannel board. Use dark blue flannel or felt for a storyboard background. Add metallic stars and a line of green felt for grass. As an option, add glitter to the angels.

Storytelling Option
Glue shapes to foam cups or cardboard tubes. Use the shapes to tell the story on a classroom table, then place them inside a cardboard box for a classroom manger set.

Song: "Go Tell It on the Mountain"

Tell the Story

In addition to the figures on the next page, use these flannelgraph pictures from the "Jesus Is Born" set (page 32): stable, Mary seated, Joseph, baby Jesus in a manger. Add the figures as you tell the story. Repeat with children reading the refrain for a story review.

Reader: *(Add shepherds, sheep, and a fire to one side of the flannel board.)* The night is dark and cold in the fields near Bethlehem. Below the starry sky, shepherds sit near their warm fire and watch their sleepy sheep. Suddenly the sky fills with light!

All: Look, look, what do you see?

Reader: *(Add angel.)* It is an angel! "Do not be afraid," the angel says. "I have good news for you. Today in the city of David the Savior has been born—Christ the Lord. You will find Him in a manger, wrapped in strips of cloth."

All: Look, look, what do you see?

Reader: *(Add other angels.)* Angels fill the sky with light and the air with their song—"Glory to God in the highest, and peace to men on earth."

All: Look, look, what do you see?

Reader: *(Take angels away.)* The sky is dark again; the air quiet and cold. The angels have gone.

"Let us go to Bethlehem," say the shepherds, and off they run to find their newborn King.

All: Look, look, what do you see?

Reader: *(Move shepherds inside manger.)* The shepherds enter the stable and find Mary, Joseph, and baby Jesus in the manger.

With joy the shepherds return to their sheep, telling everyone they meet what they saw and heard. *(Return shepherds to fire.)*

All: They saw Jesus, their Savior and our Savior from sin!

Prayer

Dear Savior, we love to tell about all You do for us. Give us words to spread the Good News that You came to save us all from sin and take us to heaven one day. Amen.

TV Screen

The Coming of the Wise Men
Matthew 2:1-12

Storytelling Set

Copy, color, and cut out the figures. Make two sets. Add glitter to the star, and if desired, to the gifts. Glue the figures to a strip of paper in the following order: standing Wise Men and star; Wise Men on camels and star; Herod; Herod's teacher; kneeling Wise Men with gifts; Jesus, Mary, and Joseph. Attach each end of the strip of paper to dowels positioned inside a "TV box." Turn the pictures through the TV screen as you tell the story.

Storytelling Options

Make stick puppets and have children move the puppets around the room to bring the Wise Men to Jesus. Or glue shapes to tubes to create puppets.

Tell the Story

Show figures as directed below.
Divide narration into parts for a story review.

(Show Wise Men.) Wise Men lived in a country, far away from where Jesus was born.

(Show star.) One night they saw a bright light in the sky. "The star is a sign that a new King is born. Let us go to worship Him," said the Wise Men.

(Show gifts.) The Wise Men took gifts of gold, incense, and myrrh and hurried on their way.

(Show figure of Herod.) The Wise Men traveled to Jerusalem, where Herod was king. The Wise Men went first to him.

(Show Wise Men by Herod.) "Where is the new King?" the Wise Men asked. "We have seen His star and have come to worship Him."

King Herod was afraid. "I do not want a new king to be born," he thought. "I want to stay king." King Herod called his own teachers. "Look in the Bible," he told them, "and see what it says about a promised King."

(Show teacher with scroll.) "The new King is to be born in Bethlehem," said the teachers.

"Go and find the new King," King Herod told the Wise Men. "Then come back and tell me where He is." The Wise Men went on their way.

(Add Mary, Joseph and Jesus.) The Wise Men went into the house and found Mary, Joseph, and Jesus.

(Show kneeling Wise Men before Jesus, Joseph, and Mary.) The Wise Men gave Jesus their gifts of gold, incense, and myrrh. An angel told them not go back to King Herod. They traveled another road to go home.

Let us join the Wise Men and worship the King.

Song: "Wise Men Traveled"

Tune: "Twinkle, Twinkle"
Wise Men by a star were led
To the Savior's baby bed.
We too come to worship Him—
Jesus Christ, our Savior King.
Wise Men by a star were led
To the Savior's baby bed.

Prayer

Dearest Jesus, our Savior King, You were born to save us from our sin. That's the best present anyone could ever receive! Like the Wise Men, we worship You and give You our praise and thanks. Amen.

New Testament Story

Cup Puppets

Jesus' Baptism
Luke 2:1-7

Storytelling Set

Copy, color, and cut out the figures. Glue the figures for Jesus and John to a foam cup, with the bottom of the cup as a base.

Glue the dove to the top of a craft stick and poke the bottom of the stick through the bottom of the cup. Keep the dove below the rim of the cup until the appropriate time in the story to push it up.

Storytelling Options

Place figures onto a flannel, magnet, or Velcro board. Or make a diorama using a cardboard box.

Song: "Jesus Was Baptized by John"

Tune: "Mary Had a Little Lamb"
When Jesus was baptized by John,
Baptized by John, baptized by John,
The Holy Spirit, like a dove,
Came down for all to see.

God the Father spoke that day,
Spoke that day, spoke that day.
"This is My Son," He then said.
"In Him I am well pleased."

I am baptized in God's name,
In God's name, in God's name.
I am baptized in God's name.
I am now God's own child.

(from *Sing-Along Praise*)

Tell the Story

Hold puppets as you tell the story. Pop up the dove as directed.

(Show John puppet.)
Dressed in fuzzy camel skin,
John told the people of their sin.
"Repent, God's kingdom is at hand,"
Said John throughout the Jordan land.
People came from every side,
"Baptize us now!" to John they cried.
(Add Jesus puppet.)
One day Jesus came to say,
"I've come to be baptized today."
"Oh no!" cried John, "This cannot be.
Rather, You should baptize me!"
But Jesus said it should be done,
And He was then baptized by John.
(Pop up dove.)
The Holy Spirit, like a dove,
Came down to Jesus from above.
God the Father spoke so clear:
"This is My Son, whom I hold dear.
I'm pleased with Him in every way."
So Jesus was baptized that day.
Now on our own baptismal day,
The Holy Spirit comes to stay.
God's special children we become,
Saved by Jesus, God's own Son.

Prayer

Heavenly Father, thank You for making us Your children through Baptism. Help us to grow in faith in You and in love for one another. Amen.

Velcro Apron

Jesus Blesses the Children
Matthew 19:13-15

Storytelling Set
Copy and color the figures. Glue them to poster board and cut them out. Glue hooked Velcro squares to the back of each figure. Use a commercial Velcro apron or cover an apron with polyester fabric.

Storytelling Option
Use the figures to make a felt book.

Tell the Story

Place figures on the apron as you tell the story. Divide parts and let children read the response for a story overview.

Reader: *(Place Jesus on one side of the apron and the mothers with their children on the other side.)* Some mothers with their children came to see Jesus. They came to Jesus' disciples.

(Place the disciples between Jesus and the mothers with their children.)

"What do you want?" asked the disciples.

All: "We want to see Jesus."

Reader: "Go away!" the disciples told them. "Jesus is too busy for children."

All: We want to see Jesus.

Reader: Jesus heard the women and children. "Let the children come to Me," He said. "I want them in the kingdom of heaven."

(Remove the disciples and move the women with children to Jesus.)

Reader: Jesus picked up the children in His arms and blessed them.

All: Jesus loves the children!

Reader: When we're baptized, Jesus blesses us with faith, forgiveness, and salvation.

All: Jesus loves us too!

Song: "Jesus Loves the Little Children"

Prayer

Lord Jesus, just like the little children in the Bible story, we come to You. And You came to us in Baptism to bring us faith, forgiveness, and life with You in heaven one day. Thank You, Jesus! Amen.

Stick Puppets

Feeding the Five Thousand
Matthew 14:15-21

Storytelling Set
Copy, color, and cut out the figures. Glue each one to a craft stick. After you tell the story, have each child make a stick figure representing themselves to hold while you tell the story.

Storytelling Options
Make a tree from a cardboard tube and use puppets to tell the story. Or make flannelgraph pictures to tell the story.

Song:
"Praise God, from Whom All Blessings Flow"

Tell the Story

First tell the story using the narration. Then have the children read the response as a lesson review.

(Show people illustration.)

Reader: "Jesus is coming," cried the people.
They ran to meet Jesus.
All: We want to see Jesus.
(Show Jesus figure.)
Reader: Jesus loved the people.
He talked to them.
He healed the sick.
He forgave their sins.
All: Jesus loved the people.
(Show Philip figure.)
Reader: It was time to eat.
"Where shall we find food?" Jesus asked Philip.
Jesus wanted to see what Philip would say.
"Eight months of work would not pay enough money to buy all these people a bite to eat," said Philip.
All: Where shall we find food?
(Show Andrew and boy figures.)
Reader: "This little boy has a lunch of five loaves and two fishes," said Andrew. "But how can that feed all these people?"
All: Where shall we find food?
(Show Jesus and boy figures.)
Reader: Jesus took the five loaves of bread.
He looked up to heaven and He prayed.
He gave them to His disciples to give to the people.
Jesus blessed the two fish.
He gave them to the disciples to give to the people.
All: There was food for all!
(Show basket shape.)
Reader: "Pick up what is left," said Jesus.
The disciples picked up 12 baskets of food.
All: To our loving God, we pray:
For gifts of food to eat each day,
For everything we need to live.
Thanks to the Lord we now will give.
In Jesus' name. Amen.

Prayer

Dear Savior, You are the Bread of life. You take away our sins and give us spiritual food. Thank You, Jesus, for saving us from sin, death, and the devil. Amen.

Stand-up Puppets

Jesus and Zacchaeus
Luke 19:1-10

Storytelling Set

Copy, color, and cut out the figures. Cut two strips of paper, making sure the strip for Zacchaeus is long enough to go around the tube. Glue both strips into loops and glue them behind the figures. Slip the loop behind Zacchaeus over the bottom of the tree so it is loose enough to slide up and down. Glue wads of green tissue paper around the top of the tube or make a treetop by cutting a construction paper circle to fit in two slits cut into the top of the tree.

Storytelling Option

Make a storytelling tube using the patterns given as guides.

Tell the Story

Add figures as you tell the story; move Zacchaeus up and down the tube to illustrate the story. Repeat with children reading the refrain for a story review.

(Show Zacchaeus.)
Reader: Zacchaeus was a tax collector. He collected taxes to give to the Romans. Sometimes he took more than he should have and kept it. People did not like him.
One day Zacchaeus heard wonderful news.
All: Jesus is coming! Jesus is coming!
Reader: Zacchaeus was a little man. The crowd was too big. How would Zacchaeus see Jesus? He had an idea. A tree stood by the road.
Zacchaeus could climb the tree.
And he did.
All: Climb, Zacchaeus, climb.
(Slide Zacchaeus up the tree trunk.)
Reader: Up went Zacchaeus.
Again the people cried:
All: Jesus is coming! Jesus is coming!
(Turn around Jesus figure.)
Reader: Jesus came under the tree and stopped.
Jesus looked up at Zacchaeus.
Zacchaeus looked down at Jesus.
"Come down, Zacchaeus," Jesus said.
       "I'm coming to your house today."
Zacchaeus hurried down.
Home he ran with wonderful news:
All: Jesus is coming! Jesus is coming!
Reader: Zacchaeus was a happy, happy man.
Jesus loved Zacchaeus.
Jesus loves us too.
Jesus forgave Zacchaeus for being greedy.
Jesus forgives us.

Song: "Zacchaeus"

Prayer

Dear Lord Jesus, You love all kinds of people, and You love me. You came to forgive the world's sins. You forgave penitent Zacchaeus and You forgive me. Thank You, Jesus. Amen.

Storytelling Tube

The Ten Lepers
Luke 17:11-19

Storytelling Set
Copy, color, and cut out the storytelling rectangles. Using the example shown on this page as a guide, cut a strip of paper to glue onto each of the other storytelling pictures. Fold back each storytelling picture and glue each strip around a tube in the following order, from top to bottom: 10 sad men, Jesus, 10 happy men, 1 happy man, and boy and girl praying.

Tell the Story
Show figures as the story is read. Repeat with children reading the refrain for a story review.

Reader: *(Turn out picture of sad men.)*
   1, 2, 3, 4, 5, 6, 7, 8, 9, 10 sick men came to Jesus.
All: "Lord, help us," they said.
Reader: *(Turn out picture of Jesus.)* And Jesus did.
(Turn back sad men; turn out happy men.)
   1, 2, 3, 4, 5, 6, 7, 8, 9, 10 sick men healed by Jesus
All: Went home well.
Reader: *(Turn back happy men; turn out one man.)*
   Only one came back to say:
All: "Thank You."
(Turn back one man; turn out boy and girl praying.)

Storytelling Option
Make and use a scroll.

Prayer
We fold our hands and pray
Unto our God each day,
To thank the Lord in heaven above
For all His gifts of love. Amen.

46

Song: "God Is So Good"

Prayer

Dear Father in heaven, Jesus healed the ten lepers. Jesus heals us too. He heals us from the sickness of our sin. Like the nine lepers, we sometimes forget to say "thank You." When we forget to say thank You, the Holy Spirit turns our hearts to repentence, and Jesus forgives us. Please help us to be like the one leper who came back to thank Jesus. In His name we pray. Amen.

Cup Puppets

The Good Neighbor
Luke 10:30-37

Storytelling Set

Copy, color, and cut out the figures and glue them to cardboard tubes.

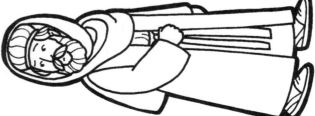

Tell the Story

Move cup puppets across the table as you read only the narration. Then, read the narration again and have children read the responses for a lesson review.

Reader: *(Place Jesus near the start of the pathway.)* "Who is my neighbor?" One day a young man asked Jesus that question. Here is the story Jesus told to answer it.

(Add injured man.) A man was walking to a town named Jericho. Robbers came and hit him. They stole his things and left him to die.

(Place picture of hurt man on the board, then move priest down path.) A priest from the temple came by. He saw the hurt man.

(Move priest to other end of path.)

All: He did not help. He walked on by.

Reader: *(Move Levite down path.)* A Levite who helped in the temple came by. He saw the hurt man.

(Move Levite to end of path.)

All: He did not help. He walked on by.

Reader: *(Move Samaritan and his donkey down path.)* A man from Samaria came by. He saw the hurt man.

All: He stopped to help. He did not walk on by.

Reader: *(Replace Samaritan and donkey with Samaritan and hurt man on donkey. Move them to the side of the flannel board.)* The man from Samaria put the man on his donkey and took him to an inn.

(Add the innkeeper.) There he paid people to take care of him.

"Who was the good neighbor in the story?" asked Jesus.

(Place first man back on the table and add priest.) The first man who walked by?

All: No.

Reader: The first man was not a good neighbor. *(Add Levite.)* Did the second man who walked by help?

All: No.

Reader: The second man was not a good neighbor. Who was the good neighbor? *(Add Samaritan.)* The man who helped?

All: Yes.

Reader: Jesus said, "Be like the man who helped."

The Good Samaritan was a good neighbor to the man who was hurt. Jesus is our good neighbor who helps us when we are sick or hurt, and when we sin. He helps us get to heaven by forgiving us.

Song: "Jesus Loves Me"

Prayer

Lord Jesus, as You have shown love to us, help us show love to others. As You have forgiven us, help us to love and forgive others. In Your name we pray. Amen.

Book

Palm Sunday
Mark 11:1-11

Storytelling Set

Cut a piece of paper in half lengthwise. Fold in half and staple the two pages together. Write "Jesus Is Coming" on the cover. Copy and cut out the shapes and glue them to the paper in this order: Children running, Jesus on a donkey, man putting down coat, mother and child waving palm branch, children singing, cross, song from following page.

Storytelling Option

Make stand-up puppets to glue to a tray for a diorama.

50

Tell the Story

Turn pages as story is read. Read the narration first. Have children take turns reading the text and refrains as a lesson review.

(Cover)
Jesus is coming.
(Picture of children running)
Hurry, hurry, the King is coming
Into Jerusalem.
All: Jesus is coming.
(Picture of Jesus on a donkey)
Clip clip, clip clop! The King is coming,
Riding a donkey.
All: Jesus is coming.
(Picture of a man putting his coat on the roadway)
Throw down your coat! The King is coming
In the name of the Lord.
All: Jesus is coming.
(Picture of a child waving a palm branch)
Wave your palm branch! The King is coming.
Run to meet Him.
All: Jesus is coming.
(Picture of children singing)
Sing hosanna! The King is coming.
Sing His praises.
All: Jesus is coming.
(Picture of a cross)
To save us from sin, the King is coming.
Sing hosanna.

Song: "Sing Hosanna to the Lord"

Tune: "Jimmy Crack Corn"
Sing hosanna to the Lord,
Sing hosanna to the Lord,
Sing hosanna to the Lord.
Jesus, come and save us.

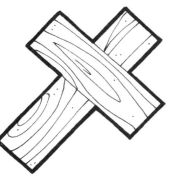

Prayer

Dearest Lord Jesus, we give You our thanks and praise for Your great mercy. Amen.

Scroll

The Last Supper
Matthew 26:17-29

Storytelling Patterns
Photocopy the figures and pictures, enlarging them as desired. Glue them along a strip of paper in the following order: Peter and John, man with a pitcher, the room, Jesus and disciples, Jesus and loaf, Jesus and cup. Glue a craft or dowel stick to each end of the strip. Roll up the strip.

Storytelling Option
Place pictures onto a flannel board.

Tell the Story

(Unroll the scroll as you tell the story.)
The time had come for Jesus to eat the Passover meal with His disciples. This meal was a prophecy about Jesus' saving work.
(Unroll figures of Peter and John.)
"Go and get ready a place where we can eat," said Jesus to Peter and John. "When you come into the city, you will meet a man carrying a pitcher of water. Follow him into the house where he goes. There say to the owner of the house, 'The Master says to you, "Where is the room where I shall eat the Passover with My disciples?"' The owner of the house will show you a large room for you to get ready."
(Unroll scroll to show the figure of a man with a pitcher of water.)
As Peter and John went into the city, they saw a man with a pitcher of water.
(Unroll picture of the room.)

They followed the man and found the room, just as Jesus had said they would. There Peter and John got things ready for the Passover meal.
(Unroll picture of Jesus at table with disciples.)
In the evening, Jesus came to the room and sat at the table with His twelve disciples. He said to them, "I wanted to eat this Passover with you before I suffer."
(Unroll picture of Jesus with bread.)
As they were eating, Jesus took bread. When He had given thanks, He broke it and gave it to His disciples. "Take and eat," Jesus said, "this is My body, which is given for you. Do this to remember Me."
(Unroll picture of Jesus with cup.)
Then Jesus took the cup. When He had drunk and given thanks, He gave it to His disciples saying, "Take and drink; this cup is the New Testament in My blood which is shed for you for the forgiveness of sins. Do this as often as you drink it to remember Me."
When Jesus and His disciples had finished the Passover meal, they sang a hymn and went to the Mount of Olives.

Song: "The Lamb"

Prayer

Jesus, our Passover Lamb, help us want to feast with You at the Lord's Supper because there You give us Your Body and Blood and take away all our sins. As we learn about this in the Bible, we are prepared for this gift. In Your holy name we pray. Amen.

Movable Strip Diorama

Garden of Gethsemane
Mark 14:32-42

Storytelling Set
Copy, color, and cut out figures. Cover the inside of a shoebox with green construction paper. Fold back the tab at the bottom of the Jesus and disciple figures and glue them to the box. Cut a slit in the side of the box to fit the angel strip through. Fold back the bush and glue it to one side of the box. Hide the angel behind the bush until needed.

Storytelling Options
Glue figures to thicker paper or poster board for more stability. Cover tree and bush with green construction paper.

Place figures on a Velcro board.

Song: "Go to Dark Gethsemane"

Tell the Story

Point to figures as you tell the story. Move the angel into the scene when directed. Divide parts for reading for a lesson review.

(Figure of Jesus and three disciples.) Jesus went with His disciples to the Mount of Olives.

"Sit here," Jesus told His disciples, "I am going to pray."

Jesus took Peter, James, and John and went further into the garden. "I am very sad," Jesus said. "Stay here and watch with Me."

(Remove picture of Jesus and disciples and add picture of Jesus praying.) Jesus went on alone. He fell on His face, and prayed, "O My Father, if it be possible, let this cup pass from Me. Nevertheless, not My will but Yours be done, Father."

(Picture of disciples sleeping.) He went back and found His disciples asleep.

"Couldn't you watch one hour with Me?" Jesus asked them. "Watch and pray that you do not fall into temptation."

(Point to picture of Jesus praying.) Jesus went and prayed a second time, then went back and found the disciples sleeping again. *(Point to picture of disciples.)*

(Add picture of angel.) Jesus went back and prayed a third time, and an angel came from heaven to strengthen Him.

(Move angel back behind bush. Point to sleeping disciples.) Jesus went back to His disciples. "The time has come for the Son of Man to be betrayed into the hands of sinners. Get up—let's go! He that is going to hand Me over is near."

While Jesus said this, Judas came leading men with swords. Judas kissed Jesus as a sign that He was the one. The men took Jesus while His disciples ran away.

Prayer

Lord God, in the garden Your Son prayed for strength to do Your will. Pardon us when we fail to do Your will. May Your will be done in our lives as it is in heaven. In Jesus' name. Amen.

Overhead Projector

Good Friday
Matthew 26:47–27:26

Storytelling Set
Trace the shapes onto dark paper and cut them out. Place them onto the overhead projector as you tell the story.

Storytelling Options
Place figures onto a flannel, magnetic, or Velcro board.

Song: "Jesus Suffered"
Tune: "Clementine"

Jesus suffered,
Jesus suffered,
Jesus suffered on the cross.
For our sins He suffered gladly.
On the cross
He died for us.

O dear Savior,
O dear Savior,
O dear Savior, You have died
In our place to give us heaven.
Thank You, Jesus,
For Your love.

(from *Sing-Along Praise*)

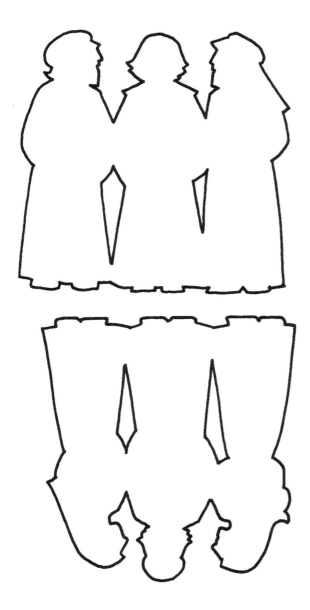

Tell the Story

Place the figures onto the overhead projection screen as you tell the story. This script is written for older children; simplify the text for use with younger students.

(Hill with three crosses.) Soldiers led Jesus from Pilate's palace to a hill outside of Jerusalem. There, at nine o'clock in the morning, they crucified Jesus. Two thieves were crucified with Him, one on each side.

"Father, forgive them," said Jesus, "for they do not know what they do."

(Add outline of kneeling soldiers.) Soldiers cast lots for Jesus' robe.

(Add outline of people.) Many people came to make fun of Jesus. The soldiers and one of the men being crucified with Jesus also laughed at Him.

The other man being crucified did not make fun of Jesus. "Lord remember me when You come into Your kingdom," this man said to Him.

Jesus said to the man, "Today you will be with Me in heaven."

(Add outline of women.) Jesus' mother, Mary, some other women, and Jesus' disciple John were close by. "Dear woman, there is your son," Jesus said to Mary. "Here is your mother," Jesus said to John. From then on John took Mary into his home.

The sun lost its light and darkness covered the land. "My God, My God, why have You forsaken Me?" cried Jesus in a loud voice.

Jesus knew that all had been done that had been foretold in God's Word. "I'm thirsty," Jesus said. A soldier soaked a sponge in vinegar, put it on a stick, and gave it to Jesus and He drank it.

Having paid in full for all our sins by His suffering on Calvary's cross, He said, "It is finished."

"Father, into Your hands I give My spirit," cried Jesus with a loud voice. Then He bowed His head and died.

(Add centurion.) "Truly, this was the Son of God," said the centurion who was standing nearby.

(Add tomb and stone.) Two friends of Jesus asked Pilate for Jesus' body and buried it. They rolled a great stone in front of the door of the tomb and left.

Prayer

Dear Jesus, thank You for dying for our sins upon the cross. Amen.

Magnet Board

Easter Morning
John 20:1-18

Storytelling Set
Glue the figures to poster board or a thick piece of paper. Color them, then cut them out. Glue magnets to the back of each shape and attach them to a metal cookie sheet as you tell the story.

Storytelling Options
Make figures into stand-up puppets to use in telling the story or have the children make a diorama to take home.

Tell the Story

Add figures to a metal cookie sheet as directed. Read the complete narration as you tell the story, then read it again for a story review with children responding as designated.

Reader: *(Place a stone in front of the door to the tomb and add soldiers; place the women on the other side of the magnet board.)*

All: Step, step, step.

Reader: *(Move women closer to tomb.)*
Three women walk to Jesus' tomb.

All: Sad, sad, sad.

Reader: *(Move women closer to tomb.)* The women are sad.

All: Who, who, who?

Reader: Who will roll the stone away?

All: Rumble, rumble, rumble.

Reader: The ground is shaking.

All: Look, look, look.

Reader: *(Add angel and remove stone.)* An angel rolls away the stone.

All: Run, run, run.

Reader: *(Remove the soldiers.)* Soldiers run away.

All: Look, look, look.

Reader: *(Add angel.)* Jesus is not here.

All: Listen, listen, listen.

Reader: To the wonderful news:

All: Jesus is alive!

Reader: The women run to tell the news to others.

All: Joy, Joy, Joy,

Reader: *(Add Jesus.)* The women meet Jesus.

All: Jesus is alive!

Song: "I Know That My Redeemer Lives"

Prayer

Jesus, You rose from the grave on Easter morning. You defeated sin and death for us. Thank You, Jesus! Help us always find joy in knowing that because You live, so will we. Amen.

Hanging Puppets

Ascension
Acts 1:1-11

Storytelling Set
Cover the inside of a box with construction paper to represent a blue sky and green grass. Glue a row of people along the bottom of the box. Cut a white cloud, with a tab and glue the cloud at the top of the box. Cut out figures of Jesus and the angels and glue a piece of yarn behind each one. Cut two holes at the top of the box and slip the other end of each piece of yarn through the holes. Start the story with Jesus at the bottom of the box and the angels at the top. As you tell the story, pull up the figure of Jesus and let down the angel shapes.

Storytelling Options
Place figures on a flannel, magnet, or Velcro board.

Tell the Story

Begin the story with Jesus at the bottom of the box and the angels at the top, behind the cloud. Move the figures as directed.

For forty days Jesus appeared to His disciples, eating and talking with them. "Go therefore and make disciples of all nations," Jesus said, "baptizing them in the name of the Father and of the Son and of the Holy Spirit, teaching them to obey everything I have commanded you. And surely I am with you always, to the very end of the age."
(Show box with Jesus figure at the bottom of the box.)
Jesus told His friends to wait in Jerusalem for the Holy Spirit to come in His fullness.
Then Jesus led His friends to a hill near Bethany. There He lifted up His hands and blessed His disciples. Then He began to rise into the sky. *(Pull up Jesus figure.)* Up, up He went until a cloud hid Him from sight.
Jesus' friends kept looking up at the sky.
Suddenly two angels appeared. *(Let down angels.)* "Why are you looking up into the sky?" they asked. "Jesus, who went up to heaven, will come again, as you have seen Him go."
Jesus' friends went back to Jerusalem with great joy, staying at the temple all the time, and praising God while they waited for the Holy Spirit to come.

Song: "You Are with Me"
Tune: "Michael, Row the Boat Ashore"

Jesus rose into the sky, Alleluia!
His friends watched and wondered. Alleluia!
Two bright angels came to say, Alleluia!
"Jesus will return this way." Alleluia!

Jesus, King of angels, stays. Alleluia!
Close by us through our days. Alleluia!
He who saved us from our sin. Alleluia!
Brings to us the hope of heaven. Alleluia!

Prayer

Dear Jesus, You went back to heaven on Ascension, but You promised to be with us always. We know that You are in Your Word and in the Sacraments. Even when we don't do as we ought, Lord, we know that You are with us and that You forgive us. Amen.

New Testament Story 61

Magnetic Puzzle

Pentecost
Acts 2:1-13, 36-41

Storytelling Set
Copy and color the puzzle and glue it to a piece of poster board. Cut out the pieces and glue magnetic strips to the back. Place the pieces on a metal cookie sheet as you tell the story.

Storytelling Option
Change puzzle shapes to ovals and glue them onto a scroll.

Prayer
Dear Father, Son, and Holy Spirit, from the very beginning of creation, You have given the world amazing gifts. You give us our very lives and all that we need. You give us Your grace and mercy. We do nothing to earn it, yet You give it freely. Thank You, God, for Your great gifts. Amen.

Tell the Story
Place puzzle pieces onto a metal cookie sheet as directed.

"Go back to Jerusalem," Jesus told His disciples before He returned to heaven, "and wait for the gift of the fullness of the Holy Spirit."

(Add puzzle piece of Jesus' disciples.)

The disciples did as He said. Twelve days later, on the day of Pentecost, they and other followers of Jesus met together in a room. Suddenly they heard a sound like a mighty wind coming down from heaven. It filled the house.

(Add puzzle piece with tongues of fire.)

Tongues of flame came to rest over the heads of Jesus' disciples. The Holy Spirit had come.

The disciples began to speak in different languages.

(Add puzzle piece with people.)

Many people had come from faraway places to celebrate Pentecost in Jerusalem. "What is that noise?" they wondered.

The people hurried to see what was happening. They found Jesus' disciples and heard them speak in different languages.

"What does this mean?" the people asked.

(Add puzzle piece with Peter.)

Peter stood and spoke. "Jesus was put to death on the cross, and raised to life again by God. Of this, we are witnesses. From the Father, Jesus received the promised Holy Spirit and poured out what you see and hear."

"What should we do?" the people asked.

"Repent and be baptized, every one of you, for the forgiveness of sins," said Peter.

About 3,000 people were baptized into God's family that day.

We are part of God's family, too, because we are baptized in the name of the Father, and of the Son, and of the Holy Spirit.

Song: "In a Room One Sabbath Day"

Tune: "Jesus Loves Me"

In a room one Sabbath day,
Jesus' friends began to pray.
Suddenly they looked around,
At the roaring, mighty sound.

Refrain: God's Holy Spirit,
God's Holy Spirit,
God's Holy Spirit,
Had come to them that day.

On each head, a flame burnt bright
Bringing each the Spirit's light.
Peter told how Jesus came
To bring salvation through His name.

Refrain.

Index

Abraham and Sarah	14
Adam and Eve	10
Angels and Shepherds	34
Ascension	60
Baby Moses	18
Daniel in the Lions' Den	28
Easter Morning	58
Feeding the Five Thousand	42
Garden of Gethsemane	54
God Made the World	8
Good Friday	56
Good Neighbor, The	48
Jesus' Baptism	38
Jesus Blesses the Children	40
Jesus' Birth	32
John the Baptist's Birth	30
Joseph and His Brothers	16
Last Supper, The	52
Miriam's Song of Praise	22
Naaman	26
Noah	12
Palm Sunday	50
Passover, The First	20
Pentecost	62
Ten Commandments	24
Ten Lepers	46
Wise Men	36
Zacchaeus	44